SAMPANS,
BANYANS AND
RAMBUTANS

A CHILDHOOD IN SINGAPORE
AND MALAYA

DEREK TAIT

AMBERLEY

ACKNOWLEDGEMENTS

Thanks to Alan Tait, Ellen Tait, Alan D. Tait and Tom O'Brien for the photos.
Check out my Singapore website at www.derektait.co.uk/sembawang.html
Also, check out my Sampans, Banyans and Rambutans blog at http://
singapore1960s.blogspot.com/

First published 2011

Amberley Publishing
Cirencester Road, Chalford,
Stroud, Gloucestershire
GL6 8PE

www.amberley-books.com

Copyright © Derek Tait, 2011

The right of Derek Tait to be identified as
the Author of this work has been asserted in
accordance with the Copyrights, Designs and
Patents Act 1988.

ISBN 978-1-4456-0315-5

British Library Cataloguing in Publication
Data.

A catalogue record for this book is available
from the British Library.

Typeset in 10pt on 13pt Sabon LT.
Typesetting by Amberley Publishing.
Printed in the UK.

INTRODUCTION

Like thousands of children who had fathers in the Navy in the 1960s, I was brought up living in Singapore and Malaya.

We moved there in January 1965, when I was just three years old. I was almost seven years old when we left. My brother, Alan was five years older than me. Although I was quite young when we were there, my memories of Singapore and Malaya are still quite strong. Who could forget the intense heat and the smells that you only found in Singapore?

Singapore, at the time, was a busy naval port with a huge British presence. The Royal Navy was stationed there for many years and didn't leave until 1971. Everything seemed to be geared towards the Navy being stationed in Singapore. The shops and the people welcomed the servicemen and their families and many businesses must have sprung up, entirely due to the influx of the Navy personnel and their families, not only from Britain but also from America, Australia and New Zealand.

We lived across the causeway at Jalan Wijaya, in Johore Bahru in Malaya, and my dad worked at KD Malaya at the Woodlands Naval Base in

Sembawang, Singapore. We lived on a newly-built estate that housed mainly naval personnel.

It wasn't uncommon for members of the Navy to be posted to Singapore and like thousands of other kids in the 1960s, I was brought up abroad on a naval estate, going to a naval school and leading a naval life.

Life was certainly different to what it was like in England at the time. The sun shone most of the time and because of the heat, school was only in the mornings. The heavy downpours of the monsoon season had us running outside when we first arrived, just to cool down. Even then, the rain was still warm! During the monsoon season the drains would flood and the water would flow up to the front door. Quite often there were violent thunderstorms that seemed to shake the whole house.

With the mosquitoes, we had to take anti-malaria tablets and we all had mosquito nets over our beds, but we'd still get bitten – they seemed to get everywhere!

The weather was constantly humid, which didn't help the bad smells that always seemed to be around. Singapore at the time was a bustling, busy city made up of three cultures; Malayan, Indian and Chinese, who all seemed to get on pretty well. The river was filled with hundreds of small sampans which people not only lived on but also plied their wares from, which included fruit, fish and other foods. There were endless shops with cheap goods that could be bartered for and also, at night time, there were markets that sold fruit, drink, goods and hot food such as Nasi Goreng, which would be cooked in front of you. It was an idyllic childhood. Not a lot to worry about, warm weather, friendly people, always lots to do and plenty of toys!

As a child in Singapore and Malaya, your memories will be perhaps of the smells, the heavy monsoon downpours, the markets, the amahs, going to school, the rickety buses with a fish left in the corner that someone had forgotten to take home for tea, the paper umbrellas that smelled of fish glue once they were wet, Tiger Balm Gardens, banyans, naval parties, Christmas, fireworks, flip-flops, the monkeys in the Botanical Gardens, Tangs, Change Alley, the toys, chit-chats, holidays etc.

Writing this book has brought back many happy memories that I thought I'd forgotten. I've tried to put together all my recollections in this book and a lot will be different from what you remember, but a great deal will probably be very similar. I hope it brings back fond memories for you too.

ONE

HOME

Our home was at 103 Jalan Wijaya, at Century Gardens, Johore Bahru, in Malaya. Century Gardens was one of the first housing developments in Johore Bahru, developed by a Johore businessman, Mr Yap Siew Cheng. At the time, it was considered a daring scheme because it was distant from the main town of Johore.

Most people living near to us in the 1960s were naval servicemen with their families, and everyone knew each other.

We had a Chinese landlord to start with, called Yap Choon Lim, but he sold the house and it was then rented to my parents by Swan Singh, who I remember wore a turban and had shoes that curled up at the end. When he was asked his name, he would say, 'Swan Singh, fly like a bird!' Mr Singh would come around with his brothers if they had anything to discuss, like the rent. I always enjoyed seeing them, maybe because of the way they dressed! They were all very friendly. There were times when I would just be looking at his curled shoes the whole time he stayed! I suppose I saw him like something out of the Arabian Nights!

At the end of our street was just jungle, far different from now, where all the land has been cleared and a Holiday Inn and shopping complex has been built. A lot of the area was covered in rubber plantations at the time.

All around the estate, there were wild dogs roaming. Some had been bought as pets and then turfed out when naval families returned home, some had been bought as puppies by drunken servicemen for their kids and been forgotten about but some were just completely wild.

Police would drive around with marksmen to shoot them in case they had rabies. I remember a wild dog standing up on my shoulders and licking my face when I was out playing and I'd heard so much about mad dogs that I ran all the way home! I stayed indoors if ever the police were after dogs as I didn't want to see them shot.

Our house was a bungalow with a garden all the way around. It couldn't have really been that big but it seemed huge to me at the time. I shared a room with my brother which had concrete floors. It was so hot that the front doors and the windows would be permanently open. We'd also have a ceiling fan going most of the time just to cool us down.

One of my favourite pastimes, with all the heat, was to stand under the hose, which was always full of holes, in the back garden to cool down. It nearly always ended up with Alan and me having a water fight, and I'd always be the one who got drenched! Before long, there were watering cans, buckets and even washing-up liquid bottles involved as we did our best to soak each other. Even David next door to us would join in. It was good fun, though, and kept us cool. Well, me anyway!

Across the way was a large house belonging to a Mr Lee. He had two wives. One night, we heard what we thought was gunfire outside. There had been trouble with Indonesian terrorists and we thought it was something to do with that, but when we got outside it was just Mr Lee letting off a load of fire crackers that were hanging over his balcony! He was celebrating Chinese New Year. The firecrackers were in long strands and were lit at the bottom and went off till they reached the top. It sounded just like gunfire! Having just arrived, we weren't used to all the fireworks going off!

Mr Lee once asked my parents over to meet Tunku Abdul Rahman, who was the first Prime Minister of Malaysia. I never knew what Mr Lee did for a job but he was quite well off and seemed to have influential friends!

Further across the road and around the corner were a row of shops. The first shop belonged to an insurance salesman who would do his exercises towards our house every morning. He would always say 'give my love to your mother!' as I walked by to the grocery shop. He had a pet monkey which was left chained to his door overnight. All the kids liked seeing it, though it seems a bit cruel now. It seemed quite happy though. The monkey was the same as the sort you got in the Botanical Gardens; they were probably just running wild further up the road, though I never saw any. One day we went around there and instead of the monkey being tied up, there was a Chinese boy tied up. I don't know what had been going on – maybe some other kids had got hold of him and thought it would be a laugh to leave him there overnight. We untied him anyway and he seemed quite relieved! The next day the monkey was back.

Further along from the insurance shop was the cold store. We got all our food from there, and it usually came with a free gift which, as a kid, I loved! I remember the washing powder always came in a bucket that would usually end up being taken to the beach. I think we ended up with loads of those red buckets in the end, but they always came in handy for something! You seemed to get something free with everything. If you bought coffee, you would get a free cup and eventually you would have a complete tea set. Every house we went to had them! Everything seemed to be recycled too. We once bought some pickles and they came in a Horlicks jar!

You could also buy pet fish in a bag from the same shop. They were all colours, and I remember we would keep them in a jam jar on the window ledge. Unfortunately they would only last a week, and nearly always ended up going down the toilet. I remember once, when we were playing in the garden, seeing one come down the open drain past us and into the main storm drain! I'd always get my pocket money, though, and the first thing I'd do with it was buy another fish! I think they had names to start off with, but this stopped once a few had died! My brother would bring back fish too, when he went on one of his fishing trips. I'm not sure where they came from; he probably fished by the Skudai. I'm sure some kids even fished in the storm drains! I know we didn't eat any of them though, and I think even the local cat turned his nose up at them! There were many weird and wonderful freshwater fish in Singapore and Malaya, including dragon fish, minnows, fighting fish, perch, catfish and many others. I'm sure that the shopkeeper told me that one of the fish we bought in a bag from him was a fighting fish, but it never seemed very aggressive to me! Maybe you needed two of them – I didn't have the pocket money!

Also around by the shops, there was always a Satay man selling cooked meats. I was never sure what the meat was; perhaps it was one of the stray dogs that wandered around the estate! We were warned not to eat it, though my brother tried it, and many of the other kids did too! It never seemed to do them any harm, though!

We loved going to the shops. There was a Coke machine outside one of them. Coke always came in a bottle and only sometimes in a can. I think 7-Up was more popular with us at the time. All the kids drank it. I loved the flavoured milkshakes too. You seemed to get them everywhere, always in coloured metal cups.

I remember that one of the shops sold toys, and I'd be mesmerised by them, especially all the tin ones. There would be tin frogs, ladybirds, robots, planes, cars etc. What more could a boy want?

There was a photographer's shop in the row too. Alan always had mum and dad's Brownie camera, and would take photos around the estate. Some of the locals weren't too happy about having their picture, taken and I think some may have lost their temper over it.

In front of our house, there was a big monsoon drain. It was quite deep, and a neighbour once got their Mini stuck in it, while trying to reverse. I think all the neighbours came out to push it out.

I got my first bike for my birthday and, while riding, one of the wheels hit the monsoon drain as I was going down the road, sending me flying into the front gate. I'd already split my head open on the front step when we first arrived, and had been taken to hospital. I can still see the x-ray machine coming down on top of me. I was alright though, and had just bashed my face a bit. My dad got the message at the naval base, but by the time it got to him it had been exaggerated and he rushed home. I remember them taking me home and talking to me, but I wouldn't answer. Then my dad said, 'Does it hurt?' And, as best as I could with my squashed face, I answered, 'Of course it hurts!'

The drains would flood during the heavy rains; sometimes the water would even flow up to our front door. At night there would be frogs and toads croaking in the drains. It was a noise, like the crickets, that you just got used to. It probably even helped to send me to sleep!

The Navy had given us an Indian housekeeper, but a lot of stuff went missing so she was sacked. The next day, I noticed a lump under the table cloth and thought it was the television cable, but then it crawled down the leg of the table and turned out to be a poisonous snake – a present from our former housekeeper! Our neighbour, Gordon Webster, came in and bashed it over the head with a broom, and it ended up in the bin! The next day my dad took it into work to ask his friend, Poon, how dangerous it was. He said as long as you weren't prone to heart trouble, you'd probably be alright! I wasn't too keen on snakes after that!

The Websters lived next door to us and had three children: David, Judith and Carol. David was my age, so was always coming over to play. We were both pre-school age when we first got there, so probably spent some of the day together on most days.

I remember the ice cream man turning up at the front on a strange contraption that was a motor bike at the front but a van at the back.

He didn't wear a crash helmet but did have a turban on! For 5 cents, you could get an ice cream, some popcorn and some free Marine Boy transfers! He would always stop outside our house because he knew I'd be first in the queue to buy something! He seemed to be there every day.

The rest of the kids in our street would all run out too, and there would be a small queue; he must have had quite a good business with all the Navy children. The ice cream would usually melt with the heat as I ate it, and I'd end up with half of it down my arm! This would happen even indoors and, as can be seen in the photo below, a saucer was used to catch the drips!

If it was hot during the day, the hose would come out again and all the kids would play under it. There was also an old tin bath which we would fill with cold water and cool off in.

The trouble with always having our shirts off is that we'd get sunburnt, sometimes badly. This happened to all the kids and you didn't realise until it was too late, especially if you'd been at the beach or in the sea all day. Nobody thought about the sun being dangerous then, so we were just out in it, uncovered, for most of the time. We must have all been brown for the whole three years we were out there!

The sun must have got to me. Here, I'm already turning red skin! We loved playing cowboys and Indians. There seemed to be more Westerns on at the time than anything else! We always wanted to be the Indians for some reason; maybe it was because there were so many Indians around us! Maybe it was just because the Indian costume was easier to make and wasn't so hot to wear.

This photo is of us playing cowboys and Indians in the front garden. I'm sure the smocks in the picture were some sort of PE kit that we had to wear at school!

Here's a picture of some naval 'pirates' at a party at our house. I remember the television being out the front and we'd all watch 'The Flintstones'! The adults would have a barbeque, drink Tiger Beer and play darts. Sometimes we would have firework displays, which were a few rockets in milk bottles, fire crackers and some Catherine wheels nailed to the fence. It doesn't sound very spectacular now, but it was great at the time.

The picture above was taken on my fourth birthday at our front door. I certainly look happy with the cake! It makes a change for me not to be barefoot or wearing flip flops!

Our windows and doors all had ornamental wrought iron work around them to stop burglars. There were stories of people with bamboo canes with fishing hooks on the end of them, reaching in through the windows to steal stuff, and this kept me awake thinking about it on several nights – though it never happened to us. The area seemed to be crime free, though the owner of the shop at the top of the hill was stabbed and killed.

He was a very jolly, fat Chinese man and all the kids liked him. I remember my brother running home to tell us.

One day, my mum called us out to the front because she thought there was a parade coming. A Chinese woman was putting candles on all the gate posts of the houses along the street. It turned out that her son had died and the candles were meant to light his way to the afterlife.

There seemed to be parties for kids all the time in the area. There were so many children that it was always one of their birthdays. We'd play traditional games like pass the parcel and pin the tail on the donkey. Toys were so cheap that everybody went home with something.

With my brother, we wandered around the estate, sometimes visiting the shops and buying the strange Chinese sweets that they sold there. We weren't really that interested in the sweets, but more so in the free toy that came with them. I think the sweets were mostly inedible anyway, but the local Chinese kids seemed to like them. Across the way from the shop was Flip Flop Hill, which my parents nicknamed because of the rubber factory beside it. I remember being on the bus going up Flip Flop Hill with my mum. It never did have the strength to get all the way up the hill and all the men would have to get off and give it a push.

Alan and I would travel down to the next estate sometimes, going over an old drainpipe. I remember Alan had some Coca-Cola tic-tacs that he'd bought at the shop. You seemed to get sweets in Singapore and Malaya that you wouldn't find anywhere else in the world. Alan dropped the tic-tacs off the drain as we crossed it. He decided to go down and get them, and cut his arm badly on the way down. It was quite a drop. I remember we had to take him home, and I wouldn't be surprised if he had to have another tetanus jab! He's still got the scar today!

Below is a photo of my brother in the front garden at Jalan Wijaya. Anyone who was in Singapore and Malaya would recognise the chair; we still had ours until the late 1990s!

While wandering around the estate, we found some wooden packing crates up by Pete Barton's house. Pete Barton worked with my dad; his two sons

went to our school at Kebunteh and one of them, Nigel, was in my class. I remember his house because it had a tall banana tree in the front garden. The tree was so big it would probably have been impossible to pick the bananas! I'm sure we tried, though! We carried the crates back home, set them up in the back garden and made a great den out of them. It seemed huge to me at the time, but probably wasn't quite as big as I remember. I can't remember if mum and dad were much bothered or not.

Sometimes we would wander up the hill across from our estate and watch the people there flying paper kites. They were all sorts of patterns from Chinese dragons to birds. They were quite hard to fly for us, but the Chinese people who were used to flying them seemed to have no trouble!

There didn't seem to be many plants or flowers, like you would get in England, in the gardens of the houses near where we lived. There were a few palm trees, but little else until you got to the jungle. It was probably too hot for most things to grow! One day, when we first arrived, I found a branch on the side of the road when we were coming back from the cold store. I took it home and stuck it in the ground in the back garden, next to the back door. Amazingly, over the next few weeks it started to grow and by the time we left after three years, it was huge! Incidentally, when I went back in 1990, it had been cut down. I wonder how big it grew eventually? I always wanted to build a tree house in it, though it probably wasn't as big as I thought!

This photo shows Alan, mum and me in the Sultan's Gardens at Johore by our car.

Dad had a Triumph Herald which was white and had a red stripe down the side. He'd bought it from Hong Heng's in Singapore. I can still remember the number plate, SP 3040, and I can still recall the smell of the inside of the car, the leather seats heated by the sun. I probably remember the smell of it so much because we always seemed to be out and about in it. It also had the luxury of a walnut dashboard.

My mum used to take driving lessons in Johore. Her instructor was called Ahmid, and he used to drive a black Morris Minor. He was always chewing betel nuts, which made his mouth very red. If my mum wasn't driving too well, he would say, 'I think you fight with husband!' or 'I take you out when you cool down!' It was scary learning to drive there, and everybody seemed to just drive down the middle with the monsoon drains each side of the road. They would even overtake you on both sides! Mum passed eventually with a few extra lessons from friends who were more used to the roads.

That Triumph Herald certainly drove some miles – we seemed to be out in it every day. I'd like to think it was still around, but it was probably scrapped many years ago!

Here's a photo of me and my dad in his tropical naval uniform before he went off to work. Every day dad left early to go to work, before it got too hot, and drove across the causeway that linked Johore with Singapore. He sometimes worked at Tanjung Rhu in Singapore. He often finished around one o'clock, and we'd meet him and go to George's Steak House at Bukit Meldrum in Johore for lunch, which was very cheap. My parents loved all the food there but, no matter what they had, I would only ever have tomato soup and then have an ice cream afterwards! The waiter knew us so well that he never asked me what I wanted, he'd just put a bowl of soup in front of me!

I don't remember my brother being so fussy about what he ate. I must have kept the ice cream industry going there with all the stuff I bought off the ice cream man who came to our door as well!

We used to sit at George's and watch as a line of ants would climb up the wall with a piece of food then, when they reached a picture, a chit-chat would suddenly appear and scoff the lot! It happened all the time. Nobody worried about the hygiene of it then and it seemed to amuse the customers! Twice a week they would have a barbeque at George's, and you would get all you could eat for two dollars and fifty cents.

Across the road from our house, there were grass cutters who had huge scythes to cut the grass with. They would cut your grass for $2 a time. They were usually women, and it always looked very dangerous as they swung the scythes over their heads and through the grass. They never seemed to injure themselves, though.

Shopping was certainly different in Singapore and Malaya. Bartering for goods was a way of life. People enjoyed trying to get a bargain and the locals expected it anyway, so put their prices up to start off with. I remember when we first got there my parents were looking for a table and chairs. They saw some they liked and asked how much they were. Sometimes, you would get ridiculously high prices because the locals knew that you had just arrived by how white you were!

The reply was 'Two Dollar Fifty, Missy!'

My mum was surprised, and turned to my dad and said 'Two Dollars Fifty!' thinking it was very cheap.

The man in the shop thought that she thought they were dear and instantly reduced the price to two dollars!

They couldn't have made much profit in the shops because they always gave all of us a drink and if you didn't have a car, they would take you and the furniture back home for free!

In the evenings, we would sometimes sit out until we were sent to bed. The Chinese takeaway man would come along and cook Nasi Goreng in front of us on his van and serve it up in banana leaves.

I remember one party at night at Les and Bette Sharpe's house. They lived around the corner from us at Jalan Wijaya. Les was setting off fireworks and hammered a Catherine Wheel to a post with a nail. When he lit it, it whizzed around, flew off and went straight up the leg of his shorts! I think he managed to put it out, though, before there was too much damage!

Here's my dad filming with his Super 8 mm camera at Kota Tinggi waterfalls. The camera was always playing up, and it must have done so on this day because we haven't got any film of the waterfalls! Kota Tinggi was about 40 miles north-east of Johore. The waterfalls were very popular with tourists and people would swim around the base of them.

There were many other attractions quite near our home. These included the Sultan's Gardens, Johore Zoo and the many beaches, including Jason's Bay.

Jason's Bay was on the east coast of Johore and seemed more popular with naval families than with locals. The beach wasn't really that great and sometimes got a bit smelly because the oxen were often led across it. That's another Far East smell that I'll never forget! We had many a banyan there, though!

The Sultan's Gardens was known locally as Istana Bukit Serene, and were part of the permanent home of the Sultan of Johore. The palace was surrounded by these spectacular gardens. We'd all go there with a loaf of bread and happily feed the Koi carp in one of the ponds in the grounds. They were quite a size and seemed to love the bread; I think it was the highlight of the gardens for all the kids.

Jalan Wijaya and Johore was certainly a great place to be brought up. I still miss it, though it seems a very long time ago now! I'd love to be sat outside the front of the house again, back in the 1960s, at night time, underneath all the stars, having a barbeque and watching the chit-chats run up and down the walls while the crickets chirped in the garden and the frogs croaked in the storm drain!

TWO

AMAHS

Most naval families had an Amah. Amah is a Cantonese word meaning 'Mother'. Our Amah was called Azizah. Amahs were paid to keep the house clean and to look after the kids. Azizah would come in the morning and would do the ironing or help around the house. She lived not far away and quite often there wasn't much to do, so my mum would send her home early. It all sounds very colonial now and almost snobbish having someone else to do your cleaning but at the time, the Navy paid for it and the local people were happy for the work and the extra money. All the kids grew attached to their Amahs. I suppose it was a bit like having a second mother!

I learned some Malay from Azizah. 'Salamat pagi' meant 'Good morning' and you would reply 'Sama-sama', which meant 'the same to you!'. Also 'Terima Kasih', which meant 'thank you'.

I remember Azizah thought we were mad when we first got there, when we ran out in the rain to cool down from the endless heat! To her, it was cold! Once, Azizah introduced us to her husband. While they were there, my mum asked Azizah if she would like some old tablecloths that she was getting rid of. She was really pleased and took them home. The next time we saw her husband, he was wearing one as a sarong!

Some Amahs would take the kids out on trips during the day to nearby places like the Sultan's Gardens.

Azizah had two of her own children; a boy called Fadzil and a daughter called Fadzilla. I don't remember the kids talking any English. They were similar ages to me though, and would always come to my birthday parties.

At night, there would be Amahs' markets. These were meant so that all the Amahs who were working all through the day would have time to do their shopping later at night. There was a great one in Bukit Timah Road. They were very colourful and the lights at night attracted huge moths. There would be all sorts of things to buy there, there would be gem traders, fruit stalls and stalls that just sold shirts. There would also be lots of hot food prepared in front of you. The smell, and it wasn't really unpleasant, is a smell I've never experienced since!

Apparently there's a service in Singapore now called 'Amahs on Wheels'! I don't know if this means you can move them around easier or that they just turn up in cars!

I sort of remember the day when we left, and saying goodbye to Azizah and her family; we were all quite close by then. It's funny how hazy your memory gets of events after such a long time!

THREE

NAVY LIFE

One of the things I liked about dad being in the Navy was that we always had lots of aunts and uncles! Of course, they were all dad's colleagues and their wives! Les Sharpe and his wife Bette lived quite nearby and had a daughter, Debbie, who was

my age and was in the same class as me at school at Kebunteh. There was also Tom Bagwell and his wife, Jean, and their kids, Robert, Ian and Linda. Robert was Alan's age, and Ian was my age and also in my class at school. Dad had a Chinese friend called Poon. How many kids can say they've got an Uncle Poon? Funnily enough, his name wasn't Poon but there was a Chinese racing driver at the time called Albert Poon and the name stuck! He even called himself Poon!

It was great when they'd all come around to our house for a barbeque or a party, even though all the kids were usually sent to bed early! Sometimes there were fancy dress parties, and I remember Les coming as James Bond. He had a diving mask with a snorkel and a plastic duck fixed to his head! I think you'd

have to watch *Dr No* very carefully to see which part he was re-enacting!

It was also great when it was one of the kids' birthdays nearby; we would all get invited and there were always lots of presents! There was always lots of food and games too.

There was a lot to do at the naval base for families. HMS *Terror* had its own swimming pool, and there was an officers' club which allowed the families of naval servicemen to use the pool. Alongside the main pool was a pool for children. Other facilities at *Terror* that families could use included a badminton court, a nine hole golf course and facilities for netball and soccer.

There was also a library by the main gate and regular cinema shows either in the chief petty officers mess, the ward room, the officers' club or in the Armada Pavilion. I remember us all going to see *Goldfinger* – I think I fell asleep! I think we saw *The Sound of Music* there too. There was also a naval base cinema at Admiralty Road East.

The naval base also had a sailing club, hairdressers, a theatre group and the Naval Base Singers, who performed two shows a year: one Gilbert and Sullivan opera and one musical comedy!

There was also a restaurant at *Terror*, and a 'men only' bar called the Tavern. Their wives were expected to drink in the Lounge part of the bar.

There were lots of wives' clubs organised and there was one near us, close to where I went to school at Kebunteh Park. The Johore Bahru wives' club met on the first and third Thursday of each month at the Garrison Welfare Centre.

KD *Malaya* also had regular film nights, and we'd often go and see them. Pete Barton would be the projectionist, but sometimes the movie reels would get mixed up so the wrong part of the film would be shown. Quite often the film just broke altogether, and everyone would have to wait until it was fixed. The NAAFI families' shop was situated outside the main gate to *Terror* and nearby was a hairdressers, a florist and a photographers. Close to the Sembawang main gate was a newsagents and a cold storage shop.

There would also be film shows, inside the base grounds, outside on warm nights for the kids. I remember watching *Peter Pan* but some kid had been sick and with the smell everyone drifted off. I'm not sure anyone stayed to see the end!

At KD *Malaya*, where dad worked with Poon, the bar was run by a Chinese man called Lingha, along with his brother, Pow. Lingha hurtled around on an old scooter, with a carrier on the back, which was usually full of curry puffs which he sold up at the officers mess. Apparently, they were delicious! My parents would sit outside on a picture night, eating curry puffs and having a drink.

Whenever dad was on duty at night, Lingha would bring him curry prawns and rice, wrapped in a banana leaf. The prawns were huge, unlike the ones you get here.

One day, dad's friend Tom Bagwell got a call from Pow to say that Lingha had died, and asked if he would go with him to collect the body. What Tom didn't realise was that they were just to be given the body as it was, and had to drive back with Lingha sat up in the back seat! Tom kept checking in his rear view mirror to see if Lingha was sitting upright! Just as well they weren't stopped by the police on the way back, but they would have probably just been used to it anyway!

In Singapore city, there was the Britannia Club for navy personnel and their families. It was on Beach Road and was run by the NAAFI. It included a snack bar and restaurant, lounge bar and tavern, games and reading rooms, a swimming pool and a sports shop.

There was also a Commonwealth Services Club on North Bridge Road.

There were also parties at night for the adults, while the kids were all at home, tucked up in bed.

Here's a bow tie and white jacket do at the naval base. On the left, smiling, is the son of the Sultan of Johore, and my parents are right of centre and their friends, Les and Bette, are to their right.

This is how our dads danced in the 1960s! This party was held at the house of my parents' friends.

FOUR

CHIT-CHATS, BOMBAY RUNNERS AND MOSQUITOES

Bombay Runners were what we now more commonly call cockroaches. I remember, when I was little and I'd just got out of the bath, that one chased me down the hallway at Jalan Wijaya! My dad had a reel-to-reel tape recorder and it packed up so he took it apart to see if he could fix it. Inside was a dead Bombay Runner, and he told us that the only thing that had kept the tape recorder going was the insect running around and around in circles!

I remember our Amah, Azizah, would just crush cockroaches with her bare feet!

Chit-chats ran up and down the walls of our house in the evening, and we loved seeing them. Chit-chat is the Malay word for lizard, and they were unusual because if you happened to catch one by its tail, it would drop off and the rest of the lizard would get away. Ideal if it was being attacked by a bird! I remember one time when there was a chit-chat in my bed. It ran off, but I wouldn't get in again until the whole bed had been checked!

The real name for a chit-chat was a flat-tailed gecko, but I'm sure all of us will always call them chit-chats! They would always come out at night and nearly always to the same spot, usually around a light, just waiting for insects and moths to appear. Chit-chats had one use, though: they ate mosquitoes! Some people even treated them as pets and gave them names. It was great sitting outside on a warm night, watching the chit-chats running about and listening to all the crickets chirping. As mentioned before, there were also the noises of the frogs and toads croaking in the monsoon drains, especially after a heavy storm.

Mosquitoes seemed to be everywhere. We had nets over our beds, but my dad was always being bitten by them. They seemed to be attracted to him far more than the rest of us! We would burn things outside called Elephant Coils that were meant to repel them. Even so, the mozzies still got my dad! It was advised to burn them in your bedrooms, too, as you nearly always slept with the windows open because of the heat.

During the day, there were lots of large ants that would quite often get in the house, probably after food. Most of the time we walked around in bare feet, and the ants used to bite with a nip. I remember if you sat down anywhere, it didn't seem long before they were heading towards you. They always seemed to be waiting at our back door to nip me if I sat down. They were quite a bit larger than the ones you normally see. They seemed to be everywhere, though. We once got a box of cereal from the cold store. I was eager to open it for the free gift but when I did, the packet was just full of ants. I wanted to fish the free gift out, but my mum took it back and they gave her another packet. The same thing happened once when I bit into a meringue and loads of ants crawled out. I think the shop keeper just laughed when my mum took it back!

There were also huge butterflies flying around too, and they would sometimes land in our garden. Of course, there was a whole manner of other creepy crawlies around, which included spiders, centipedes and weird flies called cicadas. All of them seemed to be a lot bigger than anything you got here! Some of the spiders were probably poisonous, though I don't remember coming across any of them. It was bad enough getting chased by chit-chats and Bombay Runners!

Once the sun went down, all the crickets would start making a noise. Even today, when I hear grasshoppers or crickets chirping, it reminds me of lying in bed with our mosquito nets covering us, on a hot night, and the windows open, listening to all the strange noises outside!

FIVE

AROUND SINGAPORE

One thing that really sticks in my mind about Singapore was the smell. It seemed to be a combination of rotting fruit, vegetables and raw sewerage. I'm sure if I was to smell the same smell today, it would take me straight back there!

A canal ran down the middle of the city, and there would be everything you could think of in there, including the odd dead dog!

Once you parked your car, Chinese kids would run up to you and ask for a dollar to look after it. It was worth it because if you didn't give them the dollar, you might find something missing from your car when you returned. Dad's friend Poon said that if you gave them five dollars they would also find any part you needed for your own car, probably from another parked car nearby!

Another memory of Singapore was of the noise. There would be car horns hooting, bicycle and trishaw bells ringing and the noise from the busy street markets. There'd be market sellers calling out to us, trying to sell us things or just to get us closer to their shops. There'd also be arguments going on, mainly between all the car owners, cyclists and trishaw drivers. They all seemed to drive all over the place! I don't know if there was a Highway Code in Singapore but if there was, no-one took much notice of it!

Singapore was an interesting place for a kid. There were snake charmers entertaining the crowds while street magicians would be doing tricks and making small coloured balls disappear. They would usually be by the Pedang, at the St Andrew's Cathedral compound and in front of Raffles Hotel.

I loved visiting all the markets and seeing the stall holders. There were stalls everywhere, and I particularly remember the fruit stalls and the rambutans that the stall holders would sometimes give me for free. Rambut is the Malay word for hair, and some people called them the hairy fruit. They had to be my favourite fruit in Singapore. The fruit markets overflowed onto the streets and apart from rambutans, there were durians (the smell was enough to put you off), starfruit, guava, papaya, bananas, pomelo, mangosteens and water apples. The bananas were short and sweet, unlike the bananas you get today. It was always good to stock up on them if you were on your way to see the monkeys at the Botanical Gardens! We loved coconuts too. Just the thought that they had milk inside seemed amazing to us. It didn't taste much like milk, though, and the coconut was so hard to break it probably just ended up being kicked around the garden.

There was all sorts of junk available from the stalls too. All the sort of stuff I loved as a kid. It was cheap too! Anything was available, including cheap toys, kites, paper umbrellas, hats, furniture, watches, Chinese lanterns and all manner of other things.

I don't think we ever came back without something. Of course, it was fun just bartering and trying to get a good price.

Everyone seemed so friendly as well. Maybe I just got more attention, being a small fair-haired kid, but the stall holders always seemed eager to please. I suppose all the naval families made a big difference to how much they sold. I think a lot of the markets would have been catered towards them at the time. There were certainly a lot of souvenirs available that I wouldn't have thought anyone local would have normally bought!

All the taxis were made by Mercedes. There was never a shortage of transport; if you couldn't get a taxi, there was always a bus or perhaps even a rickshaw.

The locals seemed to be fascinated by my fair hair. When we pulled into a garage, they would say something like, 'nice hair'; they seemed amazed by it. I didn't mind, though.

None of the garages were self-service and someone would come out, fill your car up, check the oil and wipe down the windscreen. Then, when you paid, you usually got a free gift. All the kids liked the Esso garages because you got free 'Put a Tiger in your Tank' badges, cups and tiger tails. Every car seemed to have a tiger tail tied to its aerial at the time!

Catching a bus in Singapore was an experience, too. Sometimes, we would catch the bus from Johore across the causeway and into Singapore. There would be live chickens running around, to keep them fresh, and huge fish, still moving, wrapped in newspaper. The smell wasn't great, but we seemed to just get used to it! Of course, none of the locals ever formed a queue to get on a bus; everyone just piled on at once and the ones that couldn't get on would cling to the back!

This photo shows the busy area of Chinatown, with all its vendors selling their wares out on the street. These would have included furniture, wooden carvings and a whole manner of goods. The goods were very cheap here but

even so, the sellers were still open to bartering. This scene features bicycles, trishaws and a VW camper with the impossible task of trying to drive through to the other end. Chinatown was situated off South Bridge Road, between Maxwell Road and the river. Chinese New Year celebrations would be great to watch here, especially the parades and lion dancing.

Once in the main part of the city, there would be traffic everywhere. I remember lots of men on scooters wearing turbans. Some wore their coats back to front when on motor bikes, but I was never quite sure why. You were meant to drive on the left, but it seemed like a free for all. As I said earlier, cars would overtake on both sides. I remember my dad's car getting hemmed in and scratched while we were in the traffic. There must have been a lot of dented cars around. There were certainly plenty of accidents.

Here's a photo of New Bridge Road showing the many cars and buses that passed through this way. On the right is an Esso sign. All the garages seemed to be either Esso or Shell and all the kids, as mentioned before, kept an eye open for them because of the many free gifts they gave away! Also on the right is a huge advert for Ovaltine, both in English and Chinese. It's hard to imagine, with the heat, that Ovaltine would have been that popular in Singapore! There's also a big box of cigarettes in the background which appear to advertise Rothmans.

If you look carefully at this picture, you'll see a feature that appears in many of the other photos of Singapore at the time – washing hanging out of windows on long bamboo poles!

Sudden downpours weren't uncommon in Singapore. In the monsoon season, everyone would have a Wanchai Burberry, which was the name then for the paper parasols you could get for a dollar. Wanchai was a place in Hong Kong where a lot of the umbrellas were originally made. Once they were wet, though, they would stink of the fish glue that held them together. Once the rains had passed, a lot of them ended up in the bin! Probably only the Brits kept them for souvenirs!

The storms seemed quite violent at times, with loud claps of thunder and bursts of lightning, but often they would clear as quick as they had come and the sun would be out again. The downpours seemed to enhance the smell of the place, though there were certainly some smells that were stronger after a storm! There were two monsoon seasons. The Northeast Monsoon occurred between September and March and the Southeast Monsoon occurred between June and September.

Trishaws, which had a bicycle on the front, would wait to pick up anyone who wanted a tour around the city, or to be taken back to their hotels. If they thought you were interested, they would ring their bell. Even if you weren't interested, they would still try and negotiate a good price! The bumpy ride was probably far more exciting than taking one of the Mercedes taxis, but not so comfortable!

Down on the waterfront were hundreds of tiny boats that filled the river. These were known as sampans, bum boats or tongkangs and they would ply their trade on both banks of the river, loading and unloading cargoes. Some wooden sampans had outboard motors to make them faster. The crowded houses on both sides of the river were said to make the place look like a beehive.

With the food and raw sewage in the river, it was a haven for rats. I probably saw more rats on the waterfront in Singapore than anywhere else, though, thinking about it now, they must have been everywhere.

Singapore River was highly polluted at the time, with rubbish from the markets, waste from street hawkers and vegetable sellers, oil spills and other waste water from boats. In 1977, the Prime Minister, Lee Kuan Yew, decided to clean up the river. There was massive resettlement of squatters and relocation of hawkers. Refuse was collected daily, and the river was dredged of all the waste that had piled up over the years. Most of the small boats disappeared and today, the river is much cleaner and many species of marine life have returned. Singapore today is a very clean city, and so is the river, but it seems the end of an era now that all the once-famous sampans have disappeared.

In the evening in Singapore, there would be the Amahs' markets too, and I can still remember the smell of the Kerosene lamps and the paraffin heaters. We used to go to one on the Bukit Timah Road. My mum bought two round green chairs there for the equivalent of five shillings. They lasted for years, even back in England!

Here's a photo of the Britannia Club on Beach Road in Singapore, which was set up for members of the forces and their families for recreation and social purposes. It was also known as the NAAFI Club or the Brit Club, and was opposite Raffles Hotel. Inside, there was a swimming pool and in the back room was a giant Scalectrix set, great for the kids though I think it was mainly used by naval personnel. Around and above the swimming pool was a huge balcony, where we'd all eat and get drinks. There were high diving boards too, though a lot of people didn't have the courage to go on them! Certainly not me!

Still in Singapore, here's a photo of my brother and our next-door neighbour, Carol Webster, entering a fancy dress competition as Red Indians. This picture was probably taken at HMS *Terror* in Sembawang. They hadn't intended on entering the competition but decided as it was starting, so my mum and her friend Barbara quickly got some crepe paper from the NAAFI shop and made up these outfits. They came second and the two boys on the right won. I preferred Noddy and Big Ears, but they came third!

Back in the city, there were many parades and religious festivals going on all the time. One I wasn't too keen on was the Thaipusam Festival. This involved someone carrying a 'Kavada' over their shoulders which pierced their body with long needles. I probably had nightmares afterwards! It was a very important Hindu festival, though, which started at Serangoon Road and finished at the Chettiar Temple at Tank Road. The piercing by needles was meant to show that the devotees were seeking forgiveness for their sins from their gods. Other religious customs and traditions included Ramadan and the celebration of Chinese New Year. I loved Chinese New Year because of all the fireworks and fire crackers that were let off. There would also be Chinese dragon dancing in the streets, and it was all very colourful and interesting to watch.

At night time in Singapore, the place would come alive again with outside markets selling cooked food and stalls selling all manner of things.

This scene shows the very popular Change Alley. Elsewhere, streets would be shut off while vendors sold their wares. Market stalls also sold many live animals, such as chickens. This was considered 'fresh' in Singapore. They also sold animals for pets, such as birds in cages. They'd probably been caught not long before. Also for sale were coloured fish, dogs and cats. You could probably even buy a monkey there, but I'm not sure if it would have been for a pet or for dinner!

I've certainly never seen anything like it since and Singapore, unfortunately perhaps, has now been vastly cleaned up.

Here's a picture of cars parked by Collyer Quay. They all look pretty dated now, but these were top of the range to our dads back then! Collyer Quay was near to the river, close to Raffles Place and Clifford Pier.

Here's a photo of the busy North Bridge Road showing many 1960s cars and a few locals riding scooters. None of them ever seemed to wear crash helmets! I'm not sure if this is a one-way street, or that's just how they used to drive!

These two photos show Bugis Street, which was near to Chinatown. There was food and goods available, and a couple of outside bars set up by rat infested drains. Perhaps it was more famous for the local men who paraded up and down here dressed as women! I can't say I ever saw any, though!

This photo shows Hock Lam Street, which was a side street between North Bridge Road and Hill Street.

A fruit-seller selling his wares at night time. Market stalls like these overflowed onto the roads all over Singapore at the time. Looking at this photo, it's easy to recall all the sounds and smells from that time.

Another view of Chinatown, clearly showing all the clothes and washing hanging out on bamboo poles.

If you wanted to get away from the hustle and bustle of Singapore, there was always the Botanical Gardens. With all the different types of plants and the added attraction of the cheeky monkeys, it was an ideal place to have a picnic and get away from the main part of the city.

SIX

TIGER BALM GARDENS

Tiger Balm Gardens was an early sort of theme park with grotesque, huge, brightly-coloured statues that depicted Chinese mythology and Purgatory, sometimes in graphic detail. There was another one in Hong Kong. The gardens were completed in 1937 by two brothers who made their name selling Tiger Balm Oil and Ointment. The brothers also had a priceless collection of jade, which was on display at The House of Jade in Nassim Road. The gardens were a popular attraction for all the naval families, and also the locals who would go there in their hundreds at the weekend or during public holidays.

We loved going and I liked climbing on all the statues, which everyone did. It's probably frowned upon now! There were signs up telling you to keep off the exhibits, but I think these were mostly in Chinese. If any of the Haw Par family are reading this – it wasn't me who broke it! What kid could resist it anyway?

At the entrance there was a huge statue of a gorilla, and there probably isn't a kid who lived in Singapore in the 1960s that hasn't got his photo taken in front of it. The path leading up to the gardens had the sea on the left, and as you entered there was a massive stone pagoda entrance, again brightly coloured, with a large picture of a tiger at the top and Chinese writing down the sides.

Below the tiger were the words, 'Tiger Balm Garden'. This had been changed from the previous wording, which read, 'Haw Par Villa' , probably because of the large influx of naval personnel from Britain, America, New Zealand and Australia.

In the 1960s, Tiger Balm Gardens was beside the sea at Pasir Panjang. Nowadays, so much land has been reclaimed in Singapore that, strangely, the sea is nowhere to be seen! The park has also reverted back to its original name, Haw Par Villa.

I remember all the brightly-painted statues of frogs, strange sea animals and mammals. There was also a huge Buddha statue, and people would rub its belly for luck!

Near the beginning of the park, there were two statues of fighting Sumo wrestlers, and further along was one of a wise old Chinese man complete with a grey beard.

This hat is still in the park (I didn't break it!), but in a different location.

Aw Boon Haw, known as the 'Tiger Balm King', originally built the gardens as a magnificent residence for his brother, Aw Boon Par. Together they'd made their fortune by creating an analgesic balm. Haw Par Villa in English translates to the Villa of the Tiger and Leopard.

The park was then created, to preserve Chinese values and way of life. This incorporated Chinese legends, history, folklore and mythology. Morality tales and battles between good and evil were also shown. I'm not sure where the giant gorilla fitted into all this, though!

Here's a photo of a statue of a female Chinese dancer which seems to appear in many photos taken at the time.

Further around, there was also a torture chamber, in statue form, and we were warned not to go in there. I never wanted to, but I think my brother ventured in. It was meant to contain scenes of Hell in various sculptures!

Also in the park there were statues of kangaroos, hippos and other marine life. All, again, were brightly painted.

As you can see from this picture, all the animals weren't to scale. Imagine finding one of these in a monsoon drain!

As I said earlier, you were meant to keep off all of these displays but nobody seemed to take much notice!

I thought at the time that Tiger Balm Gardens was a huge place, but going back in 1990, I found it had been extended, although it seemed a lot smaller. A lot of the statues had been moved around and it almost seemed like a different place. Of course, with the sea no longer there, it made it appear to be in a different location. I never did see the huge statue of the gorilla that was there in the 1960s; I hope that it hadn't been destroyed, but perhaps it had just been moved elsewhere.

My dad shot his first roll of cine film at Tiger Balm Gardens. We still watch it today, though it's not very clear and a bit dark. Cine was the latest thing, especially when used with colour film. Dad's camera was always going wrong. He'd probably bartered at Change Alley to get a good deal! It's still great to watch though.

The top photo shows my favourite attraction in the gardens – the gorillas! One of them still stands in the park today, although his teeth have been filed down and he appears to have a smile on his face! The photo below shows the pagoda entrance which was painted in vibrant gold and red, with the tiger at the top being painted a bright orange colour.

SEVEN

SHOPPING AND CK TANG'S

C. K. Tang was very Chinese looking in its architecture. It had pagoda eaves and stone lions guarding the front entrance. They sold just about everything that anyone could want but for me, the best part had to be the toy department. The tin toys were amazing, especially the robots. Some stood about two feet high and fired guns, and even talked!

Tang's was a great place to get furniture too. You could haggle on the price and they would deliver it free, no matter where you lived, and you always seemed to get some sort of free gift. Downstairs they sold the dearer items, such as carved statues and furniture, and as you got further up, everything got cheaper! My favourite part was the cheap part!

They also sold oriental curios, carvings, objects made out of ivory, linen and embroidered work, rattan-ware, leather goods and all sorts of souvenirs. They also stocked children's clothes, men's wear, Japanese pearls and had a stationery and photographic section. A whole floor near the top was devoted to camphorwood and sandalwood chests and other furniture.

C. K. Tang, who owned Tang's, started off by selling door-to-door on a hired rickshaw. By the time he died in 2000, he was over 100 years old and attributed his success to honesty, integrity and value for money. His first store opened in River Valley Road in 1934, and sold traditional Chinese handicrafts. In the 1950s, he decided to expand and bought a plot of land in Orchard Road, then an unfashionable part of Singapore. The move started the change which led Orchard Road to become one of Singapore's most famous and

popular shopping districts. Tang's was later compared to Harrods in London and Macy's in New York. Tang's leaflet described themselves as, 'Singapore's Treasure House of Old World Loveliness!'

Here's an advert showing some of the state-of-the-art appliances you could get at the time!

Another well-known shopping area in Singapore was Change Alley, where they would measure you in the morning and have a suit ready in the afternoon, all for the equivalent of 10 shillings! They would always ask you where you were from in Britain and, no matter where you said, they would say, 'I have an Uncle there!'

Another ploy was to shake your hand and not let go until you were persuaded to go in their shop! As well as tailors, where navy personnel would get their uniforms, there were shops selling all sorts of goods such as reel to reel tape recorders, the latest transistor radios, Super 8 mm cine cameras, dodgy watches, records, jewellery and just about anything you could think of. Of course, they all expected you to barter and the price would start high until you got it lower and lower, and you both felt you'd got a good deal. Incidentally, Change Alley originally got its name from the Indian money changers who ran their businesses from there.

Here's a photo of the causeway between Singapore and Malaya. I remember that my parents bought my brother a bike but, because you had to pay at the customs at the beginning of the causeway, he got out of the car and cycled it across! They'd always ask you if you had anything to declare, which my dad would answer in Malay. I wish I could remember the phrase now! It was something like, 'Taida Apa apa barang untok chucki'.

There were busy shopping centres all over Singapore. These included the ones at Raffle's Place, High Street, North Bridge Road and South Bridge Road. The stalls and markets were the most interesting for me, though, with their endless supply of cheap plastic toys and novelties, many of them just 5 cents. The next page shows a photo of the customs on the causeway between Singapore and Malaya. We passed through here regularly after visiting the shops in Singapore, before then travelling back home to Malaya.

Orchard Road was probably the most popular street for shopping in Singapore. You had C. K. Tang's at one end and a variety of stores including the cold store, where we would go in just to cool off. Further along was the Orchard Cinema, with its then-modern escalator. I remember how the doors to the shops opened as you approached them. It's something that's commonplace now, but then it seemed very futuristic. Just like in Star Trek! It was a long time before we saw them in England.

A street stall selling everything you could need for less than a dollar!

EIGHT

TOYS

Remember the tree I said I'd picked up as a twig by the side of the road and planted in the back garden? Well, here it is, not too much later!

The real reason for this photo is that it features a Cragstan talking tin robot. I'm sure many boys who were in Singapore in the 1960s had one of these, and still wishes they had it because they're worth a lot more now than the price they were then! I remember I'd seen one of these at my dad's friend's house, and then I got one for my birthday: It had four phrases when it spoke:

> 'I am the Atomic powered robot, please give my best wishes to everybody!'
> 'I'm leaving now to explore the outer limits. Goodbye, see you again!'
> 'I am a mighty man with one million horsepower of energy inside me. Do you get me now?'

And my favourite;

> 'I am bullet proof too. Ha, ha, ha!'

The last phrase I would walk around the house copying!

The toys were much more advanced than in Britain. As well as the tin robots that talked, there were ones that fired guns and flashed lights. Also, there were electronic cars, boats and planes. A lot of the toys were made of tin and they included toy animals, soldiers and clowns. All were battery-operated.

Some kids took their toys apart and found they were made out of old Coke tins! Nothing seemed to be wasted!

The toys were also a lot cheaper than they were in England. You could get all sorts like go-karts, tin pedal cars, swings, slides, anything a kid could want!

This picture was taken at the side of our house. I never did get anywhere on that horse! Tin jeeps and cars were great fun for a kid. They were all pedal-powered and with the garden clear, I was probably up and down all day!

Christmas at Tang's was amazing. The toy department, as said before, had to be my favourite part of the shop! Everything would be working for everyone to see. Looking back on it now, the toys all seemed very advanced for the time and more interesting than they are now.

Many of the shops at Christmas had their own toy department, and I think a lot of their business must have come from the many parents of naval kids just like me.

It's amazing that, at the time, these toys were so cheap! But they've become far more valuable and very collectable today. If only we'd kept them!

NINE

SCHOOL

My first taste of school was when we first got to Singapore. I was too young to go to the proper school, so I went to kindergarten. On the first day, some Chinese people picked me up in a van and took me off and put me in with a load of other kids. As far as I could gather, everyone else just spoke Chinese! At the end of the day, they forgot to take me home and there was only a couple of teachers still there who also only spoke Chinese! Somehow, they managed to get me back, but I'm not sure how they worked it out. They turned up the next day for me but I clung to the table leg and refused to go! I never did go again, and my schooling didn't start until I joined the infants at the naval base school at Kebunteh at Johore Bahru.

School wasn't really so bad. For a start, because of the heat, we only went until 1 p.m. There would be a school bus to take us there, which picked us up almost outside our door. There were older kids on the bus who would check that you were alright and that you got to school safely. Most of the teachers seemed to be naval officers. We all had to wear Royal Naval school badges (I've still got mine with my name scratched on the back!), and the younger kids had parcel labels with their names and addresses on them in case they got lost on any part of the journey to and from the school.

In the morning, we were all given bottles of milk. We had a choice between ordinary milk, chocolate or strawberry. Of course, most of the kids wanted the chocolate milk! Being on milk duty was great because you would always get first choice of the milk flavour you wanted! Some kids even preferred the white milk for some reason!

Being quite young, school was very basic for me. Probably a bit of drawing, learning to count, telling the time and reading. We also had PE in the main hall. We had black slip-on gym shoes then (no fancy trainers) and the weird smock things I mentioned earlier. Here on the Left is my school badge. It says 'RN Singapore', even though I went to school in Malaya!

Here's two photos of my brother's classes at the Juniors at Kebunteh. The tiny wooden classroom huts can be seen in the background of the top picture.

Here's a photo taken outside our house, ready to go to school. There wasn't much in those school cases, probably just a couple of exercise books and something to eat and drink! We must have got up quite early because a few times I remember sitting on the bus, and the sun would just be coming up. It was probably about 7 a.m.

We had a female teacher who all the kids liked. Once on her birthday, we all bought her a present and I remember everyone queuing up to give her our gifts. I gave her a diary; she probably had over thirty of them by the end of the day! Thinking about it now, she must have deliberately let it slip that her birthday was coming up!

Surprisingly, I remember very little about my days at school in Malaya. I remember the above photo being taken, and all the classes waiting at the top of the stairs to come down. I can also only remember a couple of the kids in this picture, Ian Bagwell and Nigel Barton.

Just down from where this photo was taken, there were playing fields. The infants and the juniors were separated by a fence but you could see through it, so sometimes at break I would talk through it to my brother in the Juniors.

A girl from the infants had eaten some wild berries in the bottom field and was taken off to hospital and one lesson we had, the headmistress, or someone, came around and told us about the dangers of eating wild fruit. It turned out that the berries weren't poisonous in the end, but we still didn't dare go near them!

There must have been all sorts of poisonous snakes and spiders in Singapore and Malaya, but I can't ever remember anyone being bitten. I definitely can't remember seeing any in the grounds of the school but, like rats, they were probably lurking very near!

This photo shows the Juniors at Kebunteh. This is my brother's class and he's on the far right in the middle row.

I've forgotten many of the lessons we took, but I do remember learning how to count and tell the time!

Also, I remember us all having to go into the assembly hall to learn to sing 'London's Burning' for some show at the school but funnily enough, I've completely forgotten everything about the show! It was probably to entertain the parents at Christmas.

We also had school photos taken in the assembly hall. It had creaky old wooden floor boards and there were posters around the wall. I remember one of them was of the three wise men visiting Jesus, but I think all the others were of elephants, tigers and other wild animals. Most of those animals probably lived nearby to our home!

At the back of the school was a bit where the infants would go and there was a bit for painting, some building blocks and a sort of Wendy House you could sit in.

I remember the first book we were ever taught to read in the infants, which had the unfortunate title *The Little Black Sambo*. Amazingly, although not very politically correct, it's still available today! Probably the reason I remember this book is because the little boy was chased by a tiger and he ran so fast around a tree that the tiger turned to butter. A strange story! We were all given it to read so probably anyone who was at the school in the 1960s remembers it.

We were also read a lot of stories from the Bible which, when I was a kid, although not religious, I really enjoyed, especially at Christmas time.

One thing I always dreaded was seeing the doctor. It must have been school time when we went for our injections at the Majeedi Clinic. My brother was scared of needles and the kid that came out before him said there was nothing to it, it just went in one side and came out the other! That was enough for Alan and there was an almighty fuss as the doctor tried to give him the injection as he kicked out. Next day, the doctor was limping! I remember going for my jabs and some of the kids crying before me. What I remember most was how my arm ached afterwards and I couldn't sleep on that side for days! There must have been a school doctor, as they always seemed to want to examine you for one thing or another! I suppose I was at the age when I was catching everything and being at school was the place to get an illness. In the three years we were in Singapore and Malaya, I had mumps, measles, German measles and a variety of other things. Most of the other kids caught the same too.

It was definitely a great place to go to school, though, and as well as the short hours, it taught me how to read, write, tell the time and also introduced me to chocolate milk!

TEN

NAVAL BASE PARTIES

The naval base seemed to have regular events and firework displays for all the naval families. For the children, there would be outside film shows. My dad's friend Pete Barton was always the projectionist and, as I said earlier, nine out of ten times the film broke, but we always had a great time.

The photo below shows me and my classmate and neighbour, Debbie Sharpe, on a float at the naval base. There were certainly lots of kids there that day. Later on, there was a fantastic firework display. One of the main attractions were the rockets. What made them different, though, was that toy soldiers would come out of the end of them and float down on tiny parachutes. All the kids scrambled around to collect them once they landed back on the ground.

Chinese New Year was also a great time at the base for fireworks and fire crackers. It usually fell at the end of January or at the beginning of February. 'Gong Xi Fa Cai' meant 'Happy New Year' in Chinese.

Because of the mixed cultures at the naval base, all the festivals were celebrated. As well as Chinese New Year, there was Ramadan, Chinese Vesak Day and Hindu Deepavali.

№ 220

*Chief and Petty Officer's Mess
K. D. Malaya*

SUMMER BALL

to be held at

8-15 p. m. Saturday 2nd September 1967

*Dancing to the Dixielanders
Lucky Ticket Draw Raffle Spot Prizes*

Dress: Formal   *Buffet 9.30 to 11 p·m·*

Here's an invite to a Summer Ball at KD *Malaya* at the chief and petty officer's mess in September 1967. There was also a Lucky Ticket Draw Raffle Spot Prize. Dad won the raffle so many times that in the end he was embarrassed to enter! One of the prizes I remember was a wooden ice bucket!

Here's a photo of my parents at the Summer Ball, which was strangely held in September!

ELEVEN

TELEVISION

The TV of the 1960s in Singapore featured programmes like *Star Trek*, *The Flintstones*, *Bewitched*, *I Dream of Jeannie*, *The Avengers*, *My Favourite Martian*, *The Man From Uncle*, *Hogan's Heroes*, *Time Tunnel*, *Marine Boy*, *Mr Terrific*, *Samurai* and *The Green Hornet* (banned in England).

Samurai had all the kids at school wanting to be Chinese warrior ninjas who, on TV, jumped backwards into trees. We even made Ninja stars out of old toothpaste tubes, which we threw around at each other. They were harmless, but to a kid they seemed like the ultimate weapon! Some kids made them out of Coke cans, which were probably a lot more lethal! My parents swore *Samurai* was in Chinese, but I understood every word. Maybe it had subtitles. It was my favourite programme, though, and I never missed a show.

Another favourite show was *Mr Terrific*, who was a sort of office worker who became a super hero after taking pills, and would then jump out of windows and fly. Everybody also watched *My Favourite Martian* and laughed when the aerials popped out of the Martian's head.

All the kids loved *The Green Hornet* too and any shows featuring super heroes like Batman and Superman. We probably re-enacted them all in the garden the next day!

There was a talent show that was on every night, and most of the contestants seemed to sing 'Fly me to the Moon' or 'I went to your Wedding'! The presenter would say, 'Tonight's prize is a lawn mower, ideal for lawn mowing!' I think it was the same prize every night.

Sometimes when we watched the TV outside the front of our house, some of the local Chinese kids would come and sit on the gate and watch it also. It was still a time when a lot of people didn't have televisions. Ours was rented from one of the local stores.

Other favourite shows at the time included *Daktari, Voyage to the Bottom of the Sea* and a cartoon series called *Gigantor. Marine Boy* and *Gigantor* were both Japanese cartoons and both very popular. *Gigantor* was the story of a boy and his gigantic robot, who would always end up fighting other gigantic robots. They were all dubbed for the American and English market, but I never noticed at the time!

Probably with being a young kid, it wasn't hard to imagine *Gigantor* as being real with all the toy robots about. Also, watching *Daktari* when there was so many wild animals nearby made it seem more real and of course watching *Voyage to the Bottom of the Sea* was what we all imagined our dads were up to when they were at work!

The 1960s seemed a great time for TV anyway, but there was something about watching all these shows in a tropical climate that made them seem somehow more real. For instance, imagine watching *Samurai* or *Daktari* in England and it's grey and pouring down outside. We'd watch the programmes, and straight after be out in the sun re-enacting them all!

I can't say that a cross-eyed lion ever wandered onto our estate, though, but it could have!

Just like our telly! Imagine watching this out in the yard!

TWELVE

WILDLIFE

Probably the best wildlife in Singapore were the monkeys in the Botanical Gardens. The Gardens were situated at Cluny Road, three miles from the centre of the city. You could catch a bus to the gate or, if you had a car, you could drive straight in. Everyone would buy bananas to feed the monkeys, and quite often they would just snatch the whole bunch out of your hand and run off with them. I was scared of the monkeys, but loved going. There was also a music pavilion and a café there.

Dad would leave the windows of the Triumph Herald down, and one day we came back to find the car full of monkeys! It looked like they were trying to drive it away!

Once he had shooed them off, he found that one of them had left him a surprise on his seat! I don't think the car smelled right for a couple of days after that!

Sadly, Singapore has been cleaned up in recent years and all the monkeys have now disappeared from the Botanical Gardens. It seems a shame because, at the time, they were one of the main attractions in the city. I'd like to think that they'd all been taken to another Botanical Gardens, possibly the one at Penang, and let go, but I somehow doubt it.

In the end, they were probably just seen like rats. We all loved seeing them though!

Johore Bahru, in Malaya, had its own zoo that was very popular, but looking back at it now, it wasn't too pleasant for the animals. They all had pretty poor, cramped cages. I remember that there was a three-legged tiger in one cage, and the reason that it had three legs was because it had been trapped by hunters and its leg was so badly injured that it had to be cut off. There was also a clapping gorilla who would clap his hands together so you would give him some food. Unlike the animals in zoos in Britain, these animals would have been born in the jungle and then captured, and would have ended their days in cages. It seems very sad now, but at the time, as kids, we loved going to the zoo. It was quite poorly looked after too, and the smell wasn't particularly great either!

There were some amazing butterflies and moths in Singapore and Malaya too. There were over 200 different species of butterflies, and some were bright yellows, blues and greens. I remember when some huge blue butterflies landed in our back garden when we first got there, and we were amazed by them. There was certainly nothing like them in England.

Atlas moths were incredible to see too. They were quite a size and common in Singapore. It was worth going to the night markets just to see them.

Other wildlife included bats. There were apparently vampire bats there, but I don't remember any! There were also squirrels, wild pigs, shrews, mice and even leopard cats. There were all kinds of frogs, including tree frogs, chorus frogs (they must have been the ones in our drains), Malayan giant frogs and even a crab-eating frog!

Here's some more wildlife: a group of bullocks being herded by a man with a stick on a bicycle! You can tell by my face how badly they smelled! I still haven't forgotten it! This photo was taken on Jason's Bay.

A group of monkeys in the Penang Botanical Gardens looking around to see who's left their car windows open!

Other wildlife included various turtles and terrapins, estuarine crocodiles and many lizards, including flying ones. The crocodiles were meant to be harmless, but I wouldn't have fancied swimming with one!

There were also many varieties of snakes. There were at least fifty different types, and these included cobras, pythons and vipers. Although some were highly poisonous, I can't remember anyone actually being poisoned or even bitten by one, but I'm sure it happened.

Of course, in Singapore city, the most common form of wildlife had to be the rat. The Singapore rat might have been common, but he even had a Latin name: Rattus annandalei! They were everywhere, and there was certainly plenty for them to feed on. They were common by the main river at night, but would also come out anywhere there was a broken drain or there was food being cooked or sold. Of course, with all the markets in Singapore at the time, this would have been practically everywhere.

There were five types of rat which included the house rat, the Malayan wood rat, the brown spiny rat, the red spiny rat and of course, the Singapore rat. I don't remember any ever coming in our house or seeing any in the garden, but I bet the monsoon drains were full of them.

THIRTEEN

SANDYCROFT IN PENANG

Many naval officers and their families spent their holidays at the leave centre at Sandycroft in Penang.

The first time we went to Sandycroft, we flew up in a plane but the second time dad drove us up in a hired Toyota. It was very cramped and his knees touched the steering wheel. It didn't have a fuel gauge either, so we were never quite sure if it was running out of petrol! It was a very long journey and I remember mum saying to look out for wild animals to keep us amused. Sure enough, we got around the corner and there were five elephants! I think they were probably shifting trees though, and weren't that wild. All the way up, we saw things on the road that at first we thought were car fan belts, but they turned out to be dead snakes! They were everywhere. We passed many rubber plantations that were owned by the Gooi Brothers. What better name for their business than 'Gooey Rubber', as we pronounced it!

One of my memories of travelling up was that we stopped at a shop because I was bursting to go to the toilet. They pointed to a hole in the floor in a room which was the toilet, but all around they were busily cutting the heads off chickens which, incidentally, carried on running around! I don't think I ever did go! Who could with all that going on? I think we probably needed a holiday after driving all that way!

Above is a shot of one of the many Gooi rubber estates on the way to Penang.

Once we were opposite Penang Island, we took the Butterworth car ferry across. It was bright yellow. It still runs today and looks much the same. It could even be the same one!

Sandycroft was set in its own grounds, about 6 miles out of George Town. It was built on a split-level system with one side being bounded by the sea, and on the other side was the road to George Town. The dining room, the ball room and the tavern were near the seashore, and the living accommodation and the reception and the barber were on a higher level. Among the activities mentioned in the Sandycroft Leave Centre brochure were fishing, tennis, football, cricket, badminton, snooker, table tennis and darts. All the amenities you would expect in the 1960s!

For 50 cents, you could hire a bike or take a coach trip to one of the attractions on the island. From the brochure, it says in your leisure time, you could visit the WVS lounge, where you could read books in the library, read magazines or listen to gramophone records! There were also three cinema shows, two dances and a tombola evening.

The above photo shows Sandycroft on the lower level. To the left are the sea and the concrete seats where we'd sit with our food from the café. Also in the picture are the yellow and red umbrellas and tables and chairs where we'd have something to eat or drink.

The nearby beach was very popular, and we'd spend our days down there swimming, messing about on the lilo or building sandcastles.

Looking at the above picture, it isn't hard for me to imagine running along these concrete paths from the beach to the café, or back to our chalet. It seems pretty empty in this picture, which was early in the morning, but it soon got

very busy once the sun came up. Further along was a jetty where you could take boat trips.

The Tavern Bar was very popular with the men, probably drinking Tiger Beer, and there was also a gift shop where, I remember buying a Corgi *Man From Uncle* car. There was no cooler TV programme then than *The Man From Uncle*!

We had a chalet overlooking the sea, near to the bay. There were fifteen family chalets. These consisted of a main bedroom and a smaller room for children. We stayed in a chalet on the higher level, and above us again was a playing field.

In the lower level of Sandycroft, closer to the beach, there were more chalets, a bar and an arcade with slot machines for the kids. If you were lucky enough to win anything on one of the slot machines, the money never came out and instead you had to find the owner and hope that nobody played the machine in the meantime. There was music played in the arcade, and two of the songs I remember were 'I'm a Believer' by The Monkees and 'Green Green Grass of Home' by Tom Jones.

I still think of that arcade when I hear those songs played on the radio!

The arcade floors were made of wood and were always covered in sand from the kids running in constantly from the beach. At the far end of the arcade was a shooting game, and the kids would wait in turns for it to be free.

Here's a photo taken in the playing field just above Sandycroft. The men played the women at football – the women won!

Above is a shot of my dad, me and my brother, Alan. This was taken by the kids' pool. On the left were more chalets, the café and the Tavern bar.

Here I am outside our chalet. We'd play football here in the evening and go down to the restaurant later for something to eat. We looked right out to the sea, and there would be some great sunsets in the evening. Incidentally, none of the chalets had toilets and you had to walk to the end of the block. It wasn't so bad in the daytime but it seemed pretty creepy at nighttime, especially with all the weird animal noises!

There was also a small park area in front of the chalets which had a swing, a slide and a see saw.

My brother making a splash in the children's pool, which was near the café. All the kids would play in here; we even took our lilo in sometimes!

The umbrellas you can see in the background, as mentioned before, were bright red and yellow and made of metal.

This picture was also taken in the childrens' pool; looks like I just lost my front teeth!

There was also a cinema there, with regular shows which would include cartoons and two films. I remember all the adults laughing at *Road Runner* and *Woody Woodpecker* when it was shown; funny how times change. I remember seeing *Born Free* there too.

One day, we were having breakfast at the café by the sea. There were a lot of people swimming, and someone suddenly shouted, 'Sharks!' Everybody ran out as quick as they could, and it was like a scene from Jaws. Suddenly, what they had seen started jumping out of the water. It turned out to be a school of dolphins! I don't think it took people very much longer before they got back in.

Penang also had its own Botanical Gardens, and I loved going for all the monkeys that were there! Actually, the place was more commonly known as the 'Monkey Gardens' to the locals. It was a great place for a picnic, but it would never be long before we had company. We always took lots of bananas and peanuts for them. The gardens were in a large valley, and at one end there was a waterfall with rivers and streams coming off it. There were also lots of birds and butterflies there, though, like most kids, it was the monkeys that really made it worth visiting for me!

Further around the island, there was the Penang Hill Railway. The railway took you above George Town, and away from the humidity of the town. There was a station at Ayer Itam, and then one half way up and another right at the top. On the way up the steep incline in the funicular railway car, you'd see miles of jungle and tall bamboo. There were probably hundreds of small monkeys hidden away, though I don't remember seeing any.

The funicular railway took us 2,400 feet above sea level to the highest point on Penang. At the top, there were food stalls, souvenir shops and a hilltop hotel.

Other Penang attractions included Ayer Itam Temple (also known as Kek Lok Si Temple), which was a Buddhist temple built in tiers. Below was the Ayer Itam market, selling souvenirs, vegetables, fruit and toys etc. In the grounds were pools of turtles. The turtles were said to be over 200 years old. Visitors were allowed to feed them with fresh vegetables. They were meant to represent a symbol of long life. The monastery featured shrines, sculptures, gardens and ponds. The pagoda was known as the 'Pagoda of Ten Thousand Buddhas' and there was a narrow stairway all the way up.

The Snake Temple was at Jelutong Road, about 9 miles out of the town. The land had been donated by an English man to a Buddhist monk a century before, and a temple had been built called Fook Heng Temple.

It became known as the Snake Temple because many of the poisonous snakes around about made their way into the temple, probably to cool off, and then made their homes in the beams, pillars and shrines.

Worshippers fed the snakes with eggs, and the smoke from the joss sticks made them quite tame and apparently harmless to the people who entered the temple. By the time we went there, it was quite a tourist spot.

I remember someone draping snakes around my neck there and my mum went mad, shouting 'Get them off!' The Indian handler said they wouldn't bite because they were doped! I can't remember being much bothered, but I do remember that they seemed pretty huge to me! I don't think I got my photo taken with them in the end, and pretty soon we were off. We'd seen enough snakes at home and on the road up!

Another attraction of Penang was at Larong Burmah, Pulau Tikus. It was called Wat Chayamangkalaram, but was more commonly called the Temple of the Reclining Buddha. Outside, it was very colourful with Chinese dragons and statues at the entrance. Inside, there was a huge, gold-plated reclining Buddha. It was said to be the third largest in the world and measured 33 metres. Penang certainly was a great place to have a holiday in the 1960s.

Today, Sandycroft Leave Centre has gone and in its place is Delat School, which took over the area in 1971. For a while some of the chalets were used as classrooms, and it was still possible to imagine what it once looked like. The Tavern and the café were turned into a canteen for the students. The sea wall was constantly in disrepair, and the school arranged for truck-loads of rocks to be delivered, which the students spent two-hour shifts carrying back and forwards to repair the walls. Can you imagine that happening in England?

Sandycroft's skyline has now changed forever with high rise blocks and beach hotels. It would be great to be able to go back and find it just how it once was, and sit under those metal yellow and red umbrellas once again, drinking Coca-Cola and looking out to sea.

FOURTEEN

BANYANS

Banyans were trips taken on boats to deserted islands, but they were also just picnics and barbeques on nearby beaches. Once there, all the men would set up parachutes to sit under and everyone would bring a picnic. As well as the barbeques, there were games of cricket and football on the beach. And, of course, plenty of Tiger Beer for our dads!

I loved going on the boats, and my Uncle Les would even let me drive sometimes. Most of the time, I'd be at the back of the boat trying to catch fish with a piece of string and a coloured fishing fly. Of course, I never caught anything but it kept me quiet!

One deserted island that we arrived at had a beach covered in starfish. All the kids collected them up to take back, though most were let go into the sea.

Many of the photos here were taken on Jason's Bay, which was a couple of hours drive from Johore Bahru. We'd usually go with my dad's friends who lived near us in Jalan Wijaya.

Les would make the kids a boat or a car out of sand on the beach that would keep us happy for ages while my mum and dad and everyone would play cricket, or sometimes water ski.

A boat made out of sand at Jason's Bay. The shells on the side read 'Jason's', and the flag was made with a twig and a white hanky belonging to Les. Our parents' cars can be seen in the background.

Here's a photo of Robert Bagwell with my brother, Alan, splashing around in the sea near Jason's Bay.

This photo shows me, in my water wings, and Ian and Linda Bagwell on a lilo off Jason's Bay. My dad's friend, and Ian and Linda's dad, Tom Bagwell, is in the background. I never really liked swimming much, so it's rare to see me anywhere near the water! The sea had its perils, though, such as jelly fish, sea snakes and even sharks. I can remember seeing a jelly fish, but I never came across any of the others!

FIFTEEN

CHRISTMAS

Christmas time was a great time for kids. The naval base would put on a party, and every kid would get a present. Someone would be dressed as Santa Claus to give out the presents, and he usually arrived by helicopter on the playing fields of the naval base. It was always sunny, which seems strange now, and it wasn't until we returned back to England that I saw my first snow.

I've got photos of me at school in December and it's a lovely sunny day. It still felt like Christmas though, especially when at that age.

The base would lay on a party and all the kids would join in. There would be games and then lots of food afterwards, and also a cinema show.

I remember the present I got from the naval Santa at the Woodlands base it was a camera. I think it fell apart before we got home. The bloke playing Santa would call out everybody's names one by one and he'd hand out the

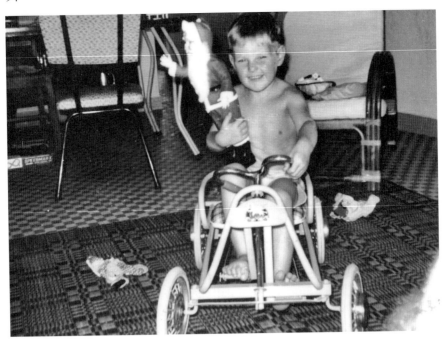

presents individually. In the evening, there would be a firework display and another cinema show.

We must have spent Christmas 1966 at George's Steak House in Johore Bahru, because we've still got the menu. Good to see that there was ice cream available! Also on the menu were roast turkey, mince pies and christmas pudding with brandy sauce, just like being in England!

I loved all the decorations going up; there were some great ones in the shops in Singapore. All the streets would be decorated in the main city.

It was great, too, just putting up the decorations in our own home and decorating the Christmas tree and hanging up cards as the sun shone outside. I loved getting up in the morning in December just to open another door on the advent calendar; it's funny how times change!

There was the anticipation too at school as it got closer to Christmas and there were Nativity plays put on, which all the little kids like me would enjoy watching. I think that the teachers even played parts sometimes.

Christmas morning was great, though, with all the fantastic toys you got there. As I said earlier, there was a toy shop around the corner in Johore Bahru and all year there were things I would hope I would be getting. The great thing was though, and what made it more exciting, was that at the time, I still believed in Father Christmas! Not sure how he got down the chimney, though, as we didn't have one. I remember the excitement of the night before, hanging up stockings, writing to Santa and then going to bed but not being able to sleep.

Everybody coming together at the naval parties at Woodlands certainly made it, though.

SIXTEEN

COMING HOME

I look glum in this photo, taken in the driveway of our home at Jalan Wijaya, but thought that it probably best shows how I should have felt about returning back to England. Actually, at the time I wasn't that bothered; it was just another adventure to me!

Incidentally, the real reason I look glum in this photo is because my brother took it and I wanted to take it!

It seemed strange heading back to England, though. I'd hardly known a life other than being in Singapore and Malaya. It was a totally different way of life. No more all-year-round sunshine, no more naval life and no more going to school just until 1 p.m. Eventually, I even missed the mosquito nets and the chit-chats!

I remember the flight home, maybe because one of the stewardesses poured hot coffee down my back! My dad had got hold of some of the British coinage to show us. It was in the pre decimal days, so there were huge pennies, halfpennies, florins and half crowns. They all seemed very big to me as the Singapore coins were very small and lightweight in comparison.

Also, to entertain us, there was a man who made paper origami animals and Chinese lanterns on the way back. He was just a passenger, but it was amazing what he made out of paper. For years after I thought he was Robert Hardin, the man off the TV who had his own Origami programme, but my parents thought it wasn't. Some of the paper animals I kept after we came back to England.

There was something to look forward to in England, though. Three years previously, all our toys and games had been packed into storage before we left. Some I could still remember, and was looking forward to seeing them again!

When we arrived back in England, we stayed with my gran at Seaham in Durham. The weather was terrible. It was freezing cold and was snowing badly. It was so windy that a workman's hut flew by us! I'm sure it was probably at this point that we all wished that we could get straight back on the plane and go home to our little house at Jalan Wijaya!

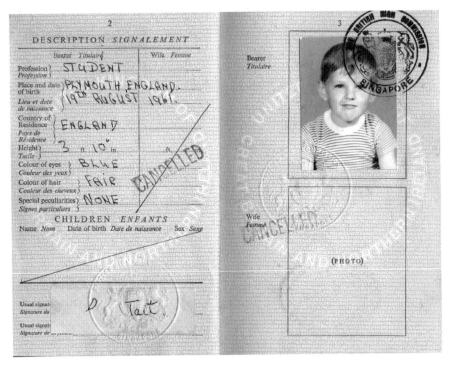

FURTHER READING

Memories of Singapore and Malaya by Derek Tait (Driftwood Coast Publishing 2007).

More Memories of Singapore and Malaya by Derek Tait (Driftwood Coast Publishing 2009).

Monsoon Memories by Derek Tait (Driftwood Coast Publishing 2010).